Series 117

This is a Ladybird Expert book, one of a series of titles for an adult readership. Written by some of the leading lights and outstanding communicators in their fields and published by one of the most trusted and well-loved names in books, the Ladybird Expert series provides clear, accessible and authoritative introductions, informed by expert opinion, to key subjects drawn from science, history and culture.

The Publisher would like to thank the following for the illustrative references for this book:
Pages 11, 27 & 37: Wikimedia Commons

Every effort has been made to ensure images are correctly attributed, however if any omission or error has been made please notify the Publisher for correction in future editions.

PENGUIN MICHAEL JOSEPH

UK | USA | Canada | Ireland | Australia
India | New Zealand | South Africa

Penguin Michael Joseph is part of the Penguin Random House group of companies
whose addresses can be found at global.penguinrandomhouse.com

 Penguin
Random House
UK

First published 2023

001

Text copyright © James Holland, 2023

All images copyright © Ladybird Books Ltd, 2023

The moral right of the author has been asserted

Printed in Italy by L.E.G.O. S.p.A.

The authorized representative in the EEA is Penguin Random House Ireland,
Morrison Chambers, 32 Nassau Street, Dublin D02 YH68

A CIP catalogue record for this book is available from the British Library

ISBN: 978–0–718–18656–2

www.greenpenguin.co.uk

The War in Burma 1943–1944

James Holland

with illustrations by
Keith Burns

Ladybird Books Ltd, London

Early on Sunday morning, 6 February 1944, Brigadier Geoffrey Evans had just reached his new post: 9th Brigade headquarters in the Arakan in north-west Burma. He was to be serving under Major-General Frank Messervy, the fearless commander of 7th Indian Division, which was in turn part of Fourteenth Army. Part of a three-division front, strung out between dense jungle and hills, they were separated from the neighbouring 5th Division by a long ridge of peaks known as the Mayu Range. A single narrow track, the Ngakyedauk Pass, had only just been completed, roughly hacked out across this mountain chain via a number of treacherous hairpin bends. This was the only link to the western coastal part of the Arakan.

No sooner had Evans reached his new command, however, than he received a horrifying signal. 'Early this morning,' he was told, 'the Japs overran Frank Messervy's headquarters at Laung Chaung. Nobody knows whether he or anybody else got away.' Laung Chaung was to the north; the Japanese were supposed to be to the south. It was vital, Evans was told, that the division's administrative area – a clearing in the jungle a mile or so to the north of 9th Brigade HQ, and the division's supply dump – be saved.

Evans neither knew where the administrative area was, nor had a clear picture of how his new brigade was disposed, but with map in hand and the rain pouring down, he set off. The situation could hardly have been worse. They were clearly surrounded, cut off, and in one of the most inhospitable places to fight in the world. And he had only a handful of men to defeat thousands of fanatical Japanese – an enemy they had yet to beat in battle. The prospects did not look good.

So far, the Burma campaign had been one humiliation after another for the British. Ignominiously pushed out in the first half of 1942, they had vowed to retake the country, and so the much-strengthened Eastern Army had thrust southwards into the Arakan at the end of that year. Barely had they crossed the border, however, than they came up against strong enemy defences, already dug into the hills. Despite throwing ever more infantry into the line, Lieutenant-General Noel Irwin's men had got nowhere, unable to master the challenges of the jungle or work out ways of breaking down the networks of Japanese tunnels, trenches and foxholes.

An attempt had been made to fight the Japanese on their own terms by sending a column of some 3,000 men under Major-General Orde Wingate into north-east Burma to attack Japanese supply lines. The Chindit Expedition, as it was known, had achieved little, suffered a lot of casualties and sucked up a lot of much-needed resources. In the Arakan, despite repeated attempts, General Irwin's men had made no progress at all, while in the skies the increasingly battered and obsolescent Hurricane fighter planes had also been unable to win mastery from the Oscars of the Imperial Japanese Army Air Force.

The monsoon had arrived in May and the fighting had stopped. The Japanese in Burma had been content to go on the defensive, as had the British. General Irwin had been sacked, along with a number of other senior British commanders. The last man standing was Lieutenant-General Bill Slim, who by the beginning of October 1944 was Acting Eastern Army Commander – an army as low on morale as it was on ideas about how to beat a fanatical and highly disciplined enemy in this terrible jungle terrain.

Slim was holed up at the former viceroy's lodge at Barrackpore. A large and ornate villa lying on the banks of the Hooghly River, it was hot, stultifying, and surrounded by the dense, creeping suburbs of northern Calcutta.

Despite these conditions, Slim used the time to try to work out a plan for transforming British fortunes in Burma and swiftly isolated four major challenges. The first was one of logistics in this inhospitable part of the world: the heat, the phenomenal amount of rain, the almost total lack of modern infrastructure along the Burma front, the distances involved and the terrain all conspired against the modern, mechanized army.

The second was to train this army to a level where they could effectively take on the Japanese – no easy task for a force made up mostly of conscripts and volunteers drawn from a hugely religious and ethnic diversity. The third was to substantially improve the health of the army, which was struggling in an area rife with malaria, dysentery and a host of other horrible diseases. And the fourth was dramatically to improve the army's disastrously low morale and rebuild a sense of belief and confidence.

Which was the toughest challenge was hard to say. Each was big enough, but collectively the task facing Slim and British fortunes in the area was Herculean.

The diversity of Eastern Army was enormous. There were Brits, Punjabis, Kashmiris, Pathans, Gurkhas from Nepal, as well as Sikhs, Hindus and Muslims. These required as many as thirty different ration scales each day – a huge amount of food to find, and especially so along an 800-mile front with only a handful of roads, two railway gauges and a number of rivers to cross.

The British and American war chiefs also recognized that South-East Asia urgently required both greater supplies and a change at the top with the introduction of a Supreme Allied Commander South East Asia in line with other Allied commands. The man they chose was a 43-year-old cousin of King George VI, Admiral Lord Louis Mountbatten.

Mountbatten's appointment raised eyebrows to say the very least, but he was dashing, glamorous, well connected, and the polar opposite of the archetypal moustachioed, silver-haired British Indian Army general. Just the man, in fact, to reassure the Americans and to bring a dose of much-needed energy.

Slim and Mountbatten first met on 22 October 1943, soon after the new Supreme Commander's arrival in South-East Asia. Mountbatten immediately liked the sound of what Slim was telling him and, against all protocol, there and then appointed him as permanent army commander with a mandate to transform his new command and the promise of full backing. In a signal of new intent, Slim also asked whether the name of his army might be changed. Mountbatten agreed. Eastern Army became Fourteenth Army. A new era had dawned and with it, they hoped, a change in Allied fortunes.

Slim immediately set to work on the solutions. Because of the lack of stone, kilns were set up and a brick road built from southern Bengal into the Arakan. Chinese were brought in to establish duck farms near the Burma front south of Imphal in the north-east, while goats, sheep and chickens were also reared locally where possible. Vast areas were turned over to the production of vegetables, while more dehydrated food was supplied from India. Further roads, like the Ngakyedauk Pass, were hastily constructed by army engineers.

Slim also quickly set about resolving the dire number of casualties lost to sickness. So far in 1943, 120 men had been pulled out of the line through illness for every one suffering combat wounds. Malaria had struck 84 per cent of those in Eastern Army per year. Dysentery also ravaged most men at some point. The answer was no longer to send them back to hospitals far from the front but to establish new Malaria Forward Treatment Units – tented hospitals just behind the front line. Those suffering would reach these within 24 hours rather than disappearing to Calcutta and elsewhere. Once better, they would be sent straight back to the front. What had before meant months out of the line could now be resolved in a couple of weeks. Taking malaria tablets also became compulsory, as did wearing long trousers and shirts with the sleeves rolled down.

Training was also much improved. Everyone was to be instructed in jungle-warfare techniques – whether infantry or service corps, such as cooks and drivers. They were taught to use the jungle to their advantage and not to fear it.

Slim's biggest anxiety, however, was that of low morale. Fear of the Japanese soldier was high. He had become a superman – vicious, almost inhuman, maliciously cruel and savage. Tales of captured British soldiers being used for bayonet practice or beheaded were rampant. Compounding the problem was a feeling of not being appreciated back home. They had become the 'Forgotten Army'.

Slim knew he had to reverse this corrosive malaise. The improvements in training, supplies and food played a big part, but so too did regular visits by both him and Mountbatten. A message of growing confidence and self-belief was delivered by them to each and every man in person.

Air power was also critical. Back in 1942, Lieutenant-General Harold Alexander, who had safely led the British out of Burma, had identified a way to defeat the Japanese. The enemy moved so fast by travelling light and resupplying using captured material. The answer was to stand firm, come what may, and deny the Japanese this bounty. With supplies dropped from the air, stubbornly holding ground ought to be possible, but to do that, control of the skies was needed. The Japanese Army Air Force had to be neutralized first.

The trouble was, British Hurricanes were evenly matched against Japanese Oscars and not fast enough to catch enemy reconnaissance planes known as Dinahs. The answer was to send over precious Spitfires, far superior in speed and rate of climb. To do so from Britain was a further enormous logistical challenge, but in September 1943 the first of these precious aircraft arrived and more soon followed.

Each newly equipped squadron was pulled out of the line and given intensive further fighter training at Amarda Road, south of Calcutta, while new Wireless Observer Units were established on the ground at 20-mile intervals all along the Arakan border and into the Chin Hills, with radio links to fighter control. Enemy aircraft could now be intercepted, and by superior aircraft too.

The rewards were not long in coming. Three Dinahs were shot down in November, as well as a growing number of Oscars. Then, on New Year's Eve 1943, the fighter pilots of 136 'Woodpecker' Squadron, in their Spitfires, attacked twelve enemy bombers and nine fighters, destroying or badly damaging every one for the loss of no pilots of their own. In the air, at any rate, the British had at long last got the better of the Japanese.

While the British were reorganizing their command structures, building up strength and training, the Japanese were also making ready for offensive operations of their own. And ever since the end of the last Arakan battle and the arrival of the monsoon, the man beating the loudest drum for action had been the commander of Japanese Fifteenth Army, General Renya Mutaguchi.

A tough, highly experienced but arrogant general, Mutaguchi aimed to strike deep into north-east India through the Plain of Imphal, then, having captured the large stockpiles of British supplies, press on to Dimapur. He was convinced that if they could successfully take Imphal and then Dimapur, the gates to India would be open; Dimapur was not only a major British railhead, it was also the key to unlocking the mighty Brahmaputra Valley, which was wide and open and very hard to defend.

Elsewhere in the Pacific, the Japanese were losing ground, but Mutaguchi hoped that such a drive into British India would prompt an uprising and the end of the British Raj: the jewel in the British Empire's crown would become the jewel of Imperial Japan instead. At the same time, a strike into Assam would capture airfields from where supplies were being flown over the Himalayas and into China to support General Chiang Kai-shek's Chinese Nationalists. Without those supplies, the Chinese would be finished and Japan could then turn the tide of the war.

Further up the chain of command, however, there was concern that Mutaguchi's vision was far too ambitious. Instead, Imperial General Headquarters in Tokyo sanctioned an offensive into India to capture the key British town of Imphal, but the operation was to be limited. Its aim was to prevent the British from ever re-entering Burma rather than to conquer India.

Dimapur

Kohima

Imphal

Calcutta

Chittagong

MUTAGUCHI

Mandalay

Lashio

Pakokku

Meiktila

Taunggyi

Yenangyaung

Akyab

Prome

Taungoo

Bago

Rangoon

Nov 1943–May 1944

☐ - ▸ Japanese forces
☐ - ▸ Allied forces

SCALE

0   160 km

100 miles

Operation U-GO, an attack into India towards Imphal, was given the go-ahead on New Year's Eve, but for Mutaguchi's attack to succeed General Masakazu Kawabe, commander of Japan's Burma Area Army, recognized that an attack in the Arakan was needed as well in order to draw British troops away from the central part of the front around Imphal.

With Operation HA-GO, General Kawabe intended to mount a lightning strike using 55 Infantry Group, part of Twenty-Eighth Army, and commanded by Lieutenant-General Shozo Sakurai. Like Mutaguchi, Sakurai had little respect for the British. 'It's child's play,' he said, 'to smash the enemy in the Mayu Peninsula.'

First, the British 7th Division, in the middle of the line, would be surrounded, isolated and annihilated. Then they would do the same to the 5th Indian Division on the western coast of the peninsula, leaving the third British division, the 81st West African, cut off and easy prey. The British would need reinforcements and these would have to come from the centre of the front. That, in turn, would fatally weaken the British position at Imphal.

The first signs that the Japanese were on the move in the Arakan came on the night of Friday, 4 February 1944, when patrols heard and spotted Japanese columns moving forward along the Kalapanzin River to the east of the 7th Indian Division. By the afternoon of the 5th, General Frank Messervy was told by Captain Anthony Irwin, commander of an organization of local Muslim irregulars called 'V Force', that the Japanese had already reached Taung Bazaar, far to the rear.

'Don't talk such bloody nonsense, Anthony,' Messervy replied. But it was true. For all Slim's preparations, the British had been caught completely by surprise. Disaster beckoned.

On reaching the administrative region of 7th Division on the morning of 6 February, Brigadier Geoffrey Evans ordered the area to be hastily turned into a defensive stronghold, swiftly renamed the Admin Box. It was too late to bring in any reinforcements. The other two brigades of the 7th Division, to the east and to the south, were told to stay put and not give a yard. Within the Box, two squadrons of Lee tanks of the 25th Dragoons had joined the division in the previous days, having successfully made the lethal crossing over the Ngakyedauk Pass at night and without discovery by the enemy. These 30-ton beasts were equipped with a main 75mm gun, as well as a smaller 37mm and a machine gun, and that they were there at all was entirely down to General Messervy, who had successfully argued that such tanks could operate in this terrain, though many others had scoffed at the notion. Having headed north to try to save division HQ, they arrived back that afternoon, as did General Messervy himself and a number of his staff. Attacked and caught up in hand-to-hand fighting, they had managed to kill several of the enemy and then give them the slip.

Also arriving was 2nd Battalion, West Yorkshire Regiment, while already there were the brigade signals and a number of service troops, muleteer, drivers, cooks, administrative and medical staff. It was not a lot, and the entire position, featuring two lonely tree-covered hills amidst an open expanse some three-quarters of a mile square and surrounded by dense jungle-clad hills, was vulnerable to say the least.

'Your job,' Brigadier Evans told his men in the Box, 'is to stay put and keep the Japanese out.'

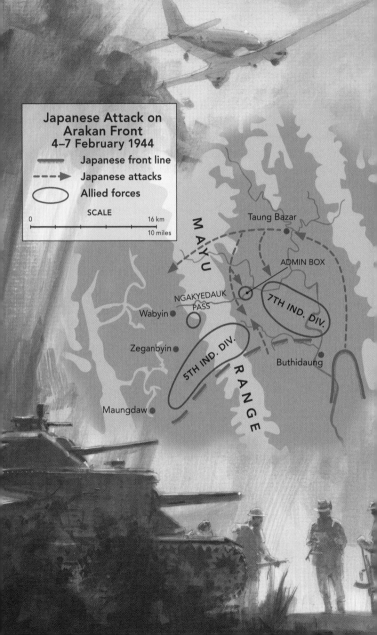

Japanese Attack on
Arakan Front
4–7 February 1944

Japanese front line

Japanese attacks

Allied forces

SCALE

0   16 km
0   10 miles

M A Y U

Taung Bazar

ADMIN BOX

NGAKYEDAUK
PASS

Wabyin

7TH IND. DIV.

Zeganbyin

5TH IND. DIV.

R A N G E

Buthidaung

Maungdaw

The Japanese first attacked the Admin Box that night, Sunday, 6 February, with tracer, screams and firing suddenly ripping apart the inky dark. They made no progress at all, but the following day cut off the Ngakyedauk Pass and then, once night fell, attacked again. This time, they caught the Medical Dressing Station, killing doctors and staff and dragging the wounded into the jungle, the screams of their victims heard by the rest of the defenders. Evans's orders – supported by Messervy – were for no man to leave his position at night under any circumstances. They were all to hold their ground.

Shocked though the defenders were, the attack on the MDS only stiffened their resolve. The following night, when the Japanese attacked yet again, the enemy were cut to pieces. In fact, night after night, the Japanese attacks failed. Several times, they advanced down the same *chaung* – dried river bed – and were slaughtered. One of the hills – Ammunition Hill – was attacked, but the tanks of the 25th Dragoons blasted the trees with their main guns and sprayed the area with machine-gun fire.

Because of the growing success of the RAF in the air, Dakotas were able to drop supplies on the beleaguered division on 8 February and into the Admin Box three days later, on the 11th. Another night, the Japanese charged across the open dried paddy fields from the north, only to be met by the machine guns of the 25th Dragoons and stopped in their tracks. The following morning, the plans for HA-GO were taken from the body of a dead officer.

The Admin Box had become a terrible place. Lying where they had fallen were hundreds of Japanese dead, and in the heat they soon began to rot. Vultures circled, while the stench became unbearable.

The defenders were suffering too – casualties were mounting with the relentless shelling by day and enemy infantry attacks by night. By 14 February there were some 400 defenders in the new 'Hospital Nullah' established after the destruction of the MDS. Yet despite these losses and despite mounting exhaustion, they were still holding on, as were the isolated battalions to the east and south, helped by the arrival of more supplies by air.

With every passing day, however, the enemy attacks were lessening as they increasingly ran short of men, ammunition and food. Sakurai's men were starving. What's more, British reinforcements were fighting their way south. On 16 February, Major Charles Ferguson Hoey, a Canadian-born company commander in the 1st Lincolns, won a posthumous VC while leading the charge against a Japanese strongpoint on Hill 315, overlooking the Box. The attack failed to take the position but the enemy were further weakened there.

By day, meanwhile, the defenders of the Box were aggressively patrolling further and further, supported by the tanks of the 25th Dragoons. On 22 February, the Ngakyedauk Pass was reopened and the wounded evacuated, while two nights later the Japanese finally pulled back, although not until 25 February was Hill 315 retaken. The Battle of the Admin Box was finally over.

Counter-attacking, the British pushed the Japanese back further. It was the first time the British had inflicted a defeat on the Japanese and, although there had been 3,506 casualties in the fighting, only a smaller number had been actually killed. The Japanese, by contrast, left 5,000 dead in and around the Admin Box and lost a further 2,000 in the fighting that followed.

The Japanese Operation HA-GO had been the first punch of a two-fisted attack designed to draw British troops to the Arakan, but despite its failure, U-GO, the invasion of India towards Imphal, was still to go ahead, as Slim's intelligence was well aware. And despite orders for a limited operation, Mutaguchi still planned to strike not only towards Imphal but further north towards Dimapur too. A fanatic, he hated the British and believed fate had handed him the chance to lead the Japanese to victory in India. Assam would be conquered, Bengal would revolt against the British Raj, then so too would the rest of the country. Britain would be forced to withdraw, humbled and humiliated. America might then make terms and Japan would win its war. He fervently believed this was his destiny: to deliver victory to the Emperor and his country.

General Slim knew the Japanese attack was coming, but not the scale or ambition of Mutaguchi's plans. That Imphal was the prime objective, though, was clear and, now familiar with his enemy, Slim knew they were expecting the British to act the way they always had – and retreat. He realized that if he did exactly that, the Japanese would think the British were the ineffective, flighty, morale-crushed force they had always been. So he planned not a withdrawal but a fighting retreat, in which the Japanese divisions would be increasingly ground down and degraded. It was certainly a bold plan, but the Admin Box had shown that his men were of a different calibre than they had been a year before. He believed they were now equal to the challenge.

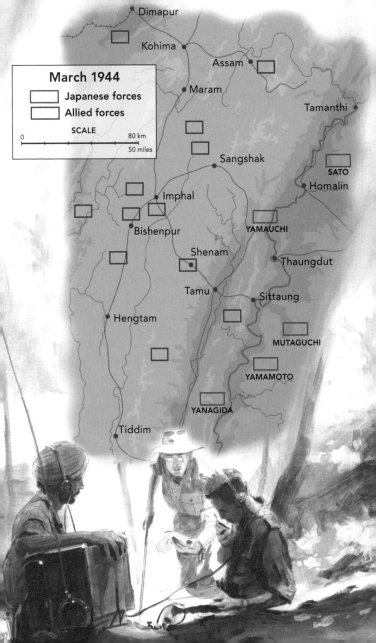

They were far better led too. Slim had personally chosen all his senior commanders. Men like Generals Stopford, Messervy, Gracey, Cowan, Briggs and Roberts were tough, tactically astute, beloved by their men and by now very experienced. Slim hoped that by the time his divisions had fallen back to Imphal, the Japanese would already have suffered badly. The enemy's lines of supply would be woefully stretched, while Fourteenth Army's would be shortened. After two years' fighting the Japanese, Slim also knew they were unlikely to retreat in a hurry, so he intended to hold them at Imphal, grind them down further, then counter-attack. And annihilate them.

The challenges of operating in this inhospitable part of the world were such that only by an emphatic victory would Fourteenth Army have enough of a free hand to re-invade Burma successfully from the north. It was, though, unquestionably a high-risk strategy. If it failed, the whole of India, and possibly even the course of the entire war against Japan, could be at risk.

In fact, Slim's plan went awry almost from the outset, with the first of several near-disasters. Protecting Imphal was IV Corps under Lieutenant-General Geoffrey Scoones. His three divisions were all far apart: one to the south-east protecting the road from Burma across the Shenam Saddle Hills, another to the south covering the other route into Burma, the Tiddim Road, while a third was in reserve around Imphal itself.

Scoones and Slim had anticipated Mutaguchi's attack beginning on 15 March, but the southern thrust up the Tiddim Road began a whole week earlier. Men from the Japanese 33rd Division had already crossed the Manipur River and were moving north and to the west of the Tiddim Road to block the British retreat.

Major-General David 'Punch' Cowan, the British 17th Division commander, swiftly realized what was happening, but Scoones discounted the intelligence of the Japanese outflanking moves. He knew it was essential they didn't withdraw too soon and so ordered Cowan to keep his men where they were. Fortunately for the fate of Imphal, Cowan ignored Scoones and ordered his men to start falling back. It was the right decision. He was the man on the spot, he trusted his own judgement and, by pulling his men back when he did, unquestionably not only saved his division, but averted disaster.

The Tiddim Road saw some extraordinary fighting – Japanese and British troops were interspersed along the road like a Neapolitan sandwich but, supported by the RAF, Cowan's men successfully fought their way back to Imphal, reaching the southern edge on 4 April and so badly mauling the Japanese 33rd Division that the enemy no longer had the strength to push on through to the city. It had been a close-run thing, but to the south, at any rate, Slim's strategy was working.

Elsewhere, however, other disasters loomed. To the south-east of Imphal ran the road from Burma over which the beaten British had retreated in May 1942. Now it was the axis of advance for the Japanese 15th Division under Major-General Tsunoru Yamamoto. Major-General Douglas Gracey's 20th Division had already prepared a series of defensive positions along the Shenam Saddle and here they made their stand.

Once again, though, the decision to withdraw was given very late and to only roughly prepared positions. The defence 20th Division put up was out of all proportion to what the Japanese had come to expect from British and Indian forces. Bitter fighting took place here – scenes of devastation likened to the battlefields of the Somme were the result.

However, while Gracey's men were successfully holding the Japanese onslaught along the Shenam Saddle, more enemy columns were bypassing them to the north, including Lieutenant-General Kotoku Sato's entire 31st Division.

Mutaguchi's men were now attacking from all around. Slim described the battle as being like the spokes of a wheel with Imphal the hub. By the beginning of April, Japanese forces were attacking down a number of these spokes – including, most worryingly, from the north. It was to the north of Imphal that the British had most of their supply bases as well as airfields – located there precisely because they were thought to be safest. Slim had intended to lure the Japanese towards Imphal, but had not meant them to get as close as they now were. To make matters worse, Sato's men were also heading towards Kohima, way to the north of Imphal. If they managed to take this shallow saddle successfully and cut the road to Dimapur, catastrophe would loom.

The 50th Indian Parachute Division arrived at Sangshak to the south-east of Kohima in mid-March. They were commanded by Brigadier Maxwell Hope-Thompson, who, at just 31 years old, was the youngest brigadier in the Indian Army. He posted his Gurkha and Indian battalions around the area, intending to acclimatize and train his men further before they were posted to the front line. Little did he realize the front line was coming to him.

The leading elements of the Japanese 58th Regiment, Sato's spearhead, clashed with C Company, 502nd Battalion, on 17 March. Surrounded, the Indians fought ferociously but were slaughtered almost to a man. During C Company's final charge, one of the officers even put a pistol to his head rather than be taken prisoner.

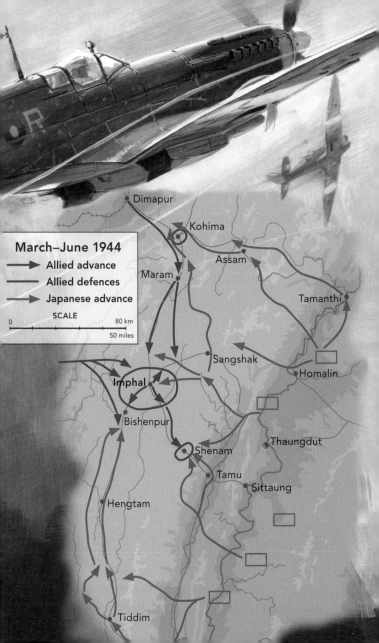

March–June 1944

→ Allied advance
— Allied defences
→ Japanese advance

SCALE
0 _____ 80 km
      _____ 50 miles

Dimapur
Kohima
Assam
Maram
Tamanthi
Sangshak
Homalin
Imphal
Bishenpur
Thaungdut
Shenam
Tamu
Sittaung
Hengtam
Tiddim

Hope-Thompson now knew he was facing a sizeable Japanese formation. Cut off, and with barely enough supplies and neither mines nor wire, both essential for strong defence, he decided to bring his men together to face the full fury of the Japanese attack. He chose the village of Sangshak to make his stand.

The first major assault on the position came on the evening of 22 March. The Japanese attack was launched as the sun was setting and straight at the dug-in Gurkhas. It was a massacre. One observer said it was like an optical illusion, with the Japanese tumbling as they all fell. Ninety men out of a 120 in the company were killed within minutes.

From then on, the Japanese shelled and mortared the defenders by day and made increasing numbers of attacks by night. Both sides were soon suffering debilitating casualties, but yet again, on the body of one Japanese officer, the complete enemy plans were found. And they showed that the main target for Sato's 31st Division was Kohima.

Incredibly, the brigade's intelligence officer managed to slip through the Japanese positions and walk all the way back to Imphal, where he handed over this golden piece of information. Meanwhile, for four days and four nights, the defenders grimly hung on.

Finally, on 26 March, after being sent a clear signal over the radio to withdraw, Hope-Thompson ordered those still standing to try to break out. At around 11 p.m., having fired the last of their mortar and artillery shells, they made a dash for it – and were entirely successful. The fighting had cost them dearly, but for all their sacrifice Sangshak had had far-reaching and decisive consequences.

Meanwhile, Slim landed at Imphal on 29 March to confer with Scoones and his senior commanders. Neither had expected the Japanese to move so quickly or on such a broad front and, since the plans captured at Sangshak had not yet reached them – although they were aware there was a major enemy force to the north – they were unsure whether the enemy was heading for the tiny hill village of Kohima or the main railhead and supply base of Dimapur.

A further urgent threat also had to be faced, as forces from the Japanese 15th Division were fast approaching Imphal from the north-east and were now just a few miles from the airfield at Kangla. Yet it was in this moment of crisis that the Allies' superior air power was about to become a decisive factor. Fleets of transport planes could, in theory, move entire brigades, and even divisions, up to the Imphal front. The trouble was, these were mostly American and were being used to fly the 'Hump' – the route over the Himalayas into China to supply Chiang Kai-shek's forces.

Fortunately, the very strong working relationship between Mountbatten and Slim had led to mutual trust. Consequently, when Slim asked for an urgent diversion of US transport aircraft to support Fourteenth Army, Mountbatten didn't hesitate, even though he should have asked permission from the US Chiefs of Staff. But he didn't. He knew he had to make a decision right now, and had the courage of his convictions to do so. Flight after flight landed at Imphal Main, bringing in the battle-hardened 5th Indian Division from the Arakan. It was the first time ever a division had been brought into battle by air alone – and they arrived in the nick of time.

Japanese troops were already on the Nungshigum Ridge to the north of Imphal when the newly arrived 5th Division first clashed with them. From Nungshigum, Imphal was in sight, and from this dominating position the enemy could launch an assault on the town. Somehow, some way, the new arrivals in 5th Division had to clear the enemy from this vitally important ridge.

On 13 April, dive-bombers and Hurri-bombers were sent to bombard the Japanese, then Indian infantry supported by Lee tanks attacked. Every one of the infantry and tank officers was killed or wounded, so it was left to the NCOs, the sergeant-majors, to continue the drive forward. And they did win the day. As they swept over the ridge, they found the bodies of over 250 dead Japanese.

The US transport fleet now remained in support of Fourteenth Army until the end of the battle, bringing in even more troops, including XXXIII Corps, to Dimapur under the command of Lieutenant-General Montagu Stopford. But while the airfield at Kangla was being saved by the heroics of 5th Division, by this time a further major battle had developed at Kohima, to the north. It was to be the fourth – and final – potential disaster to befall Fourteenth Army.

And the most serious threat of them all.

In the spring of 1944, Kohima was home to a small village of local Naga tribesmen and a handful of British buildings, not least the bungalow and tennis court of Charles Pawsey, the Deputy Commissioner for Nagaland, on Kohima Ridge. Lying on a low saddle amongst the hills, this lonely outpost between Dimapur and Imphal was defended by just 2,500 men, of whom 1,000 were non-combatants. And Sato's division was heading straight for them.

If Kohima fell quickly, General Mutaguchi intended to order Sato to drive straight on to Dimapur, which at the end of March was barely defended at all. General Montagu Stopford's XXXIII Corps was being hurried there, but until the divisions that were being flown in arrived in strength he had insufficient forces with which to defend both Dimapur and Kohima at once.

In fact, there was just 161st Brigade at Kohima, and Stopford worried that if the outpost were surrounded and defeated before the newly arriving 2nd Division reached this corner of the front, then there would be nothing with which to defend Dimapur. It was a dilemma, but Stopford feared the threat to Dimapur, lying clear of the hills and with its railhead and supply dumps, was the more serious and so ordered 161st Brigade to fall back. Slim supported his decision.

Although a logical course of action, it was the wrong one because 2nd Division was reaching Dimapur and now Kohima was terribly exposed. 'I have spent some uncomfortable hours at the beginning of battles,' Slim admitted, 'but few more anxious than those of the Kohima battle.' On 3 April, the decision was reversed and 161st Brigade turned back to Kohima. Two days later, 5 April, they had reached it, by which time some 13,000 Japanese troops were bearing down on Kohima Ridge.

Sangshak had given the defenders a crucial lifeline, however: because of the paratroopers' stand there, General Sato's men had reached Kohima a week later than planned. The question now was whether the Royal West Kents and Assams – the two battalions of 161st Brigade at Kohima – could hold out against a force ten times bigger until reinforcements reached them.

Somehow, these few defenders doggedly managed to hold on to Garrison Hill. The fighting was bitter, bloody and at close quarter. It was also witness to a number of acts of breathtaking bravery, not least that by Lance-Corporal Jack Harman.

The son of the millionaire owner of Lundy Island off the north Devon coast, Harman had preferred the ranks to a commission. Eccentric and an unlikely soldier, he was also a man with scant regard for his own safety. On 9 April, he leapt out of his slit-trench on the ridge, charged across the open ground to a Japanese machine-gun nest and, with just rifle and bayonet, killed them all. He headed back, triumphantly brandishing the Japanese machine gun above his head, only to be shot in turn. For this action, he was posthumously awarded a Victoria Cross.

By 18 April, the defenders were struggling to hold a small perimeter on Kohima Ridge when the position was split by the Japanese. It looked as if all might be lost, but then, in the nick of time, Major-General John Grover's 2nd Division finally started to arrive from Dimapur. Overnight on 20 April, with the bloodied defenders just managing to cling on, the position was relieved.

By the time 2nd Division reached Kohima, the ridge had become a scene of indescribable devastation and filth. It had been the grimmest kind of fighting imaginable: close-quarter, often hand-to-hand, and with foul smoke and the appalling stench of rotting corpses ever present.

Despite the carnage, by the third week of April all four near-disasters facing Fourteenth Army had been averted. The enemy onslaught had been successfully checked.

Although Imphal remained besieged, Slim was not especially worried and now wanted to stick to his original plan: to grind down the Japanese at Kohima, on the Shenam Saddle, on the Tiddim Road and on the road north. Exploiting Japanese weaknesses, not strengths, had always been his plan; he knew they would not dare give up, but rather would keep fighting. Slim's supply lines, however, were now secure and reinforced, whereas Mutaguchi's were worsening daily. In the numbers game the battle had become, there could be only one winner.

At Kohima, the battle continued, despite the beginning of the monsoon adding to the misery. One of those arriving in the first week of May was Major Mike Lowry, commanding B Company, the Queen's Royal Regiment. He and his men had been at the Admin Box and had now been flown in to defend Kohima, reaching it amidst the scream of shells and pouring rain.

Lowry's men were flung into the battle on Jail Hill on 11 May, attacking in the cold early dawn behind a brief barrage. 'I started the ball rolling,' noted Lowry, 'by whistling over some grenades and then we all ran forward. But the terrain was not easy, there being many shell-holes, horizontal tree stumps and the odd trench to negotiate.'

Casualties swiftly rose and they soon became bogged down just yards from the Japanese positions. Both sides began sniping and hurling grenades. 'It was,' noted Lowry, 'the nearest approach to a snowball fight that could be imagined. The air became thick with grenades, both theirs and ours, and we were all scurrying about trying to avoid them as they burst.' They held their ground, but by nightfall Lowry had just twenty-eight men left. He had begun the day with seventy-nine.

The fighting around Imphal and Kohima was among the most brutal of the war, and especially so now the monsoon had arrived. 'We were soaked all the time,' Captain Robin Rowlands, an officer in the 7/2nd Punjab Regiment, said. 'And filthy. The mud was appalling.' So was the stench, as thousands of unburied dead soldiers lay strewn over the hillsides. Japanese troops were taught that being taken prisoner was dishonourable and would bring shame upon their families, so very often they fought to the death. Most British and Indian troops were short of their normal rations, but the Japanese were starving. Malnutrition and disease went hand in hand, yet Mutaguchi was still maniacally urging his men to keep fighting. 'If your hands are broken, fight with your feet,' he exhorted them, 'if there is no breath in your body, fight with your ghost. Lack of weapons is no excuse for defeat.'

Meanwhile, back in London and Washington, Allied war leaders were getting nervous and urging Mountbatten to instruct Slim to relieve the siege of Imphal urgently. Far away from the action, they were following lines on a map in which there was little movement but a continued maximum effort of air supply.

It was certainly slow, hard fighting, and it took the British a month just to push the Japanese 10 miles down the road south of Kohima. Bitter fighting also continued south and north of Imphal, and over the Shenam Saddle too, as the Japanese were prised from one hill after the other. Yet, by fighting for every yard, the enemy was playing into Slim's hands. He wanted to annihilate Fifteenth Japanese Army here in India rather than in Burma. Supported fully by Mountbatten, he stuck to his strategy. The gradual destruction of the Japanese Fifteenth Army would continue.

By the beginning of June, it was clear the Japanese were nearly finished. Yard by yard, mile by mile, 5th Division was pushing northwards from Imphal and 2nd Division was inching ever further southwards from Kohima. On 22 June 1944, the British forces met and, at last, after sixty-four days of ferocious fighting, the road was open. That same night, the first convoy in three months drove through to Imphal. The siege was over.

In the long month that followed, with the monsoon now in full swing, the shattered remnants of Mutaguchi's once-proud army began to fall back. At the end of the Imphal battle, the remnants of the Japanese 31st and 15th Divisions retreated back through the jungle and along the roads they had swiftly advanced over just a few months earlier when they had been so confident of victory.

Now they were beaten, exhausted, ill and emaciated. Robin Rowlands was among those sent in pursuit. Along the jungle tracks, he witnessed hundreds of dead Japanese soldiers lying where they had fallen, dead from starvation, disease and exhaustion. 'It was a terrible sight,' he said. Some had even resorted to cannibalism. The retreat became known as the 'Road of Bones'.

The shattered remnants of the Japanese Fifteenth Army crawled back into Burma utterly broken as a fighting force. On 20 July, General Mutaguchi finally gave orders for the survivors to fall back across the Chindwin River, his dreams of becoming the conqueror of India gone for ever. 'It is the most important defeat the Japs have ever suffered in their military career,' wrote Mountbatten on the day the siege was lifted, 'because the numbers involved are so much greater than any Pacific Island operation.'

Imphal was certainly a superb and also a decisive victory. Had Mutaguchi reached and captured Dimapur, then India really would have been vulnerable. Bengal had recently suffered an appalling famine that had left millions dead and anti-British feeling in India was growing, especially in Bengal. The Bengalis were ripe for insurrection. If India had been lost, then the airfields from which China was being supplied would have been lost too.

Mutaguchi had been right – the battle had been the last chance for Japan to change the course of the war. It was the largest land battle the Japanese had fought up to this point in the entire war and the stakes had been enormous. At its end, the Japanese Fifteenth Army had been destroyed, just as Slim had planned.

Of the 65,000 fighting troops that had crossed into India back in March, 30,000 lay dead, rotting in the hills and jungle of Manipur and in the Naga Hills, while a further 23,000 had become casualties. Incredibly, only 600 had let themselves be taken prisoner. In all, so far in 1944, the Japanese had lost some 90,000 men fighting the British Indian Army and five entire divisions had been completely destroyed. Fourteenth Army had lost 24,000 casualties, many of whom recovered thanks to the improved medical care upon which Slim had insisted.

Hard fighting continued as Slim's forces pursued the Japanese into Burma. The long campaign of reconquest would continue into 1945, but by any judgement the year had witnessed an astonishing reversal of fortunes that could not have been remotely guessed at just twelve months before. Not only was Imphal a monumental victory for the British, it was also a complete vindication of Slim's strategy. Not for nothing has this been called Britain's greatest battle.

Further Reading

GENERAL HISTORIES

Robert Lyman *Slim, Master of War* (Robinson, 2004)

Robert Lyman *A War of Empires* (Osprey Publishing, 2021)

MEMOIRS

Jon Latimer *Burma: The Forgotten War* (John Murray, 2004)

George Macdonald Fraser *Quartered Safe Out Here* (Harvill, 1993)

Henry Maule *Spearhead General* (Odhams Press Ltd, 1961)